WHEN GOD CAME DOWN

WHEN GOD CAME DOWN

by ANDREW W. BLACKWOOD, JR.

BAKER BOOK HOUSE
Grand Rapids 6, Michigan
1955

WHEN GOD CAME DOWN

_____

FIRST PRINTING, September, 1955

LIBRARY OF CONGRESS CATALOG CARD NUMBER: 55-10435

To
Andy, Margaret, and Mike

CONTENTS

1

THE MESSAGE THAT MATTERS

And there were in the same country shepherds abiding in the field, keeping watch over their flock by night. And, lo, the angel of the Lord came upon them, and the glory of the Lord shone round about them; and they were sore afraid. And the angel said unto them, Fear not; for, behold, I bring you good tidings of great joy, which shall be to all people. For unto you is born this day in the city of David a Savior, which is Christ the Lord. And this shall be a sign unto you; Ye shall find the babe wrapped in swaddling clothes, lying in a manger. And suddenly there was with the angel a multitude of the heavenly host praising God, and saying, Glory to God in the highest, and on earth peace, good will toward men.

LUKE 2:8-14

There Were Shepherds

The most important message of history came to a group of farm-hands as they were working by night on a hillside in Palestine. The rich sheep-owners were asleep in town. The shepherds were out on the hill, tending the flocks, when the angel of the Lord brought God's message to them. Some ultra-pious folk of the day looked down upon shepherds because they were not able to keep all the ceremonial requirements of the

9

Law. A man who had to work for his living sometimes found it difficult or impossible to follow the rules and regulations of spiritual life that loomed so large in those days. A shepherd had a lonely life with his sheep and his dog. There were few comforts, many difficulties.

The angel of the Lord came to the shepherds and delivered his tidings. Rough, uneducated men received the message which is so rich and so vast there is not room in the human mind to receive it all. The scholars who have delved most deeply into the mystery disclosed to the shepherds are the first to confess their inability to comprehend it.

As you seek to understand the message, you find yourself, soon or late, dazzled by the light of mystery that surrounds the ultimate Mystery of Being — God. You can be sure the shepherds did not fully understand the good news God sent to them. Was the message therefore wasted? A professor I know thinks that Jesus made a profound mistake. Jesus brought the gospel to the farmer, the longshoreman, the store clerk. The professor thinks that Jesus should have brought the message first to the classroom. Then, when the intellectuals were converted, they could have gone out to convert the masses. But Jesus, like the angel, brought divine wisdom to be examined by uneducated people, and they taught it to the intellectuals.

The angel might have learned a lesson from us today. Whether or not the lesson is worth learning, I shall leave for you to decide. As you look at any of our large cities, you can see bright, new churches going up in our bright, new suburbs. For this, I say, "Thank God." But down in the slums the church is running away.

Today's slum was yesterday's fashionable residential district. The people who have moved away, out to the bright, new suburbs, explain that those now living round about the church building "aren't our sort of people." The shepherds weren't "our sort of people" either, but God thought them His sort of people, and He delivered to them a message that is designed to redeem poor and rich alike.

How Did God Speak to the Shepherds?

The record tells us that "the angel of the Lord came upon" the shepherds. Our dubious twentieth century is apt to raise a quizzical eyebrow upon hearing the word "angel." To most people, the word conjures up the vision of a biological impossibility having the frame of a man and the wings of an eagle. It is obvious that such a being is aerodynamically unsound. A being with an eagle's wings would need an eagle's breast muscles in order to fly. Since our misconception of an angel is ridiculous, many have decided that the whole idea of angels is ridiculous. For the poor person who lives in a one-story universe, it is.

We who believe in the spiritual dimension of reality live in a many-tiered universe. We believe that this world of molecules will pass away, in time, but that the world of the spirit is eternal. Between the ultimate Spirit, God, and man, who is the lowest order of spiritual being, there are spiritual beings whom we call angels. Angels are agents of God in carrying out His eternal purpose.

What we do not know about angels has filled many dismal volumes. In the middle ages, our fathers used to debate, with mock solemnity, the question, "How

many angels can stand on the point of a pin?" The
correct answer to the question is: "Since angels are
spiritual beings, an infinite number of them can 'stand'
on a point with no dimension." Our fathers who de-
bated the question were gently spoofing the tendency
to talk endlessly on subjects we know nothing about.
They knew they were joking, however much our con-
temporaries may have missed the point of the joke.

Possibly an angel is "seen" with the "eye" of spiritual
vision. The optic nerve may not enter the process at
all. The watchers on the hillside saw an angel, but the
record nowhere says that the sheep also saw him.
Whether or not the shepherds had a visual experience,
in the usual sense of the word, they had a profound
and meaningful spiritual experience as the angel of
the Lord delivered the message to them.

The word angel means messenger. A messenger's
place in life is to deliver the message entrusted to him,
then to fade from the picture. The message is what
matters, not the way in which it is delivered.

How Does God Speak to You?

It is quite possible that God will send His angel to
bring you a special message tonight. But the probabili-
ties are all against it. To most of us God brings His message in less spectacular ways, through nature, through
people, and supremely through the Scripture.

God Speaks through Nature. The psalmist sings,
"The heavens declare the glory of God; and the firma-
ment showeth his handiwork" (Psalm 19:1). God
created the world, and He declared it good. As man
studies His handiwork in nature, he feels near to the
mystery of God. And so it is but natural that men who

lack the light of divine revelation should turn to nature worship. In olden times people made gods of springtime, the sun, fertility, and the like. Our twentieth century pagans have retained from the distant past a standard defense gambit, "I can feel more religious out in the woods than I can in church." To this the standard Christian reply is, "So can I."

Was the Savior born so that people could have religious feelings? People had those centuries before the first Christmas. If the angel had the message straight, Jesus Christ was born to save us, not to make us feel religious. The religious feeling of God-in-nature is part of the total picture in Christianity. When one attempts to make it the whole picture, one's faith is tragically incomplete.

Let me illustrate natural religion at work in my life. One evening I saw a sunset, out in the blood-soaked Solomon Islands. We had been through an air raid earlier in the day. It was a light bombing. Only two of our buddies were killed. But that sort of thing leaves a person feeling depressed. At dusk, as the sky was filled with "scarlet running over on the silvers and the golds" we all stopped our work and looked to the west. I do not know what the sunset meant to my friends. To me it "sang" aloud, "Glory to God in the highest." But that was not all. There was a timeless calm that seemed to say, "If only man would get in tune with the glory of God, he could know this peace eternally." That was a deep religious feeling. Did I just imagine that God was speaking to me through the sunset? I believe that God was at work in nature, not merely in my imagination. But notice how incomplete His message. Natural religion is wonderful, as far as it goes. But it is lacking in moral content, and it lacks the message of salvation; for it leaves one grappling hopelessly with that insurmountable "if."

God Speaks through Human Nature. God speaks to people through other people. He brings divine wisdom to bear upon many problems through the agency of human wisdom. For example, God is just, and He has implanted a sense of justice in man. The human agents of justice — policemen, lawyers, judges — are but imperfect instruments of divine justice. And yet the Scripture says of the civil magistrate, "He is the minister of God to thee for good" (Rom. 13:4). The Apostle was writing about the law-enforcing agents of the Roman Empire. He remembered well that some of these agents had yielded to the demand that they crucify Jesus. Human justice is far from perfect. It is a reflection, but twisted and distorted, of divine justice.

God speaks to people through people. He has implanted in the human soul some knowledge of His will for man. A trace of this knowledge remains in every human heart. And so, wherever you may go, you can find some sort of religion and some sort of morality. As you study the religious and moral systems of the world, you decide there is no belief too fantastic to find a believer somewhere, and no moral practice so vile that somewhere man has not considered it good. Men have held and expressed every possible belief about God and human duty. In all these contradictory beliefs there must be elements of truth, but how can one determine from the tangle of confused reports which to believe? Taking a majority vote is the best possible way of deciding upon a course of political action, but it is a dangerous way of trying to establish truth about religious and moral issues.

God Speaks through the Bible.   The Bible is a collection of books that were written by men. It was not engraved upon plates of gold by a committee of archangels. The Bible is a human document, written by mortal hands, in ink that could fade, upon parchment that could crumble into dust. Ages before the first word of the Bible was written, parts of it were handed down by oral tradition. After the discovery of writing, the human authors of the Bible wrote in their own tongues — Hebrew and Greek. They wrote on three continents, over a period of more than a millennium. The writers were princes, soldiers, farmers, poets, store-keepers, professors, and philosophers, and their writings reflect their different human vantage points. Since there is so much variety in the Bible, one might confidently predict that it would be a grab-bag of religious confusion; and one would be totally wrong.

The Bible is more than the word of man. The Bible is God's Holy Word. Through its pages, God has been speaking to ever-increasing numbers of people, teaching them about Himself and His will for man. The Bible is more than the views of the prophet Isaiah and the Apostle Paul about spiritual matters. The Bible is God's inspired, authoritative Word to man, given through such men as Isaiah and Paul. The Bible shows a unity of theme and development that can be explained only by looking beyond the human authors to the divine Author, who revealed Himself and His will to chosen human agents, over a period of centuries. Finally the revelation was made perfect through the One whose birth was proclaimed to the shepherds.

Well-intentioned people have misused the Bible. It is not a crystal ball for predicting the next move of the men in the Kremlin. It is not a good-luck charm to ward off the normal hazards of human existence. It does not answer all of man's questions — you will search its pages in vain for the multiplication table. It is not a substitute for human intelligence. It is divinely intended to offer to you the answer to life's central question, "What must I do to be saved?" (Acts 16:30).

While a few foolish people have been abusing the Bible, in ways that God never intended, millions upon millions have been seeking, and finding, the solution to man's problem in its pages. In more than a thousand different languages today, men are reading, "Unto you is born this day in the city of David a Savior, which is Christ the Lord."

God's Message to the Shepherds

The angel told the shepherds of a child who was born in Bethlehem, whom they might find "wrapped in swaddling clothes, lying in a manger." When they had received the message, the shepherds said to one another, "Let us now go even unto Bethlehem, and see this thing which is come to pass, which the Lord hath made known unto us." And having decided to go, they went. They set a good example for the rest of us. They heard the truth about Jesus, they accepted the message in faith, then they investigated.

"This day." We shall leave to the historian the precise date of the Savior's birth. Thanks to Quirinius, the matter is not likely to be settled in our time. There has been so much unprofitable wrangling about the year when Jesus was born that some have branded the Gospel account a myth designed to give a birthplace in Bethlehem to one who was called the Nazarene. Like most attempts to explain away the Bible, this one creates more problems than it solves. Luke describes events that made him shudder. The census that brought Mary and Joseph to Bethlehem was ordered by a Roman emperor, and carried out by a despised Jewish king. When people invent myths, they arrange their facts to glorify the hero. Faithful historians put down the glorious and the tragic alike. And no Christian ever rejoiced that Jesus was born in the filth of a stable. What Luke records is strong indirect evidence that he is writing history, not fiction. Even so, we do not know the precise day or the exact year when the events took place.

"In the city of David." The city of David is Bethlehem, a sleepy little country village, lying about five miles to the south-southwest of Jerusalem, in a fertile farming area. When the wise men came to Jerusalem, following the star, they asked where the King of the Jews was to be born. The sages in the Temple confidently replied that Bethlehem was the birthplace. They were interpreting a prophecy of Micah who wrote, seven centuries before, "Thou Bethlehem Ephratah, though thou be little among the thousands of Judah, yet out of thee shall he come forth unto me that is to be ruler in Israel; whose goings forth have been from of old, from everlasting" (Micah 5:2). Micah is giving much more than geographical information. He uses Bethlehem as a symbol descriptive of the coming Christ.

David was the most popular king of Jewish history. He was a shepherd boy who guarded his father's sheep on the hills near Bethlehem. The prophet Samuel came to the farm one day, and anointed the young shepherd to be ruler over Israel. In Micah's day — some three centuries after David — most of the people who lived in Bethlehem were dirt farmers, living in desperate economic insecurity. The wealthy and powerful lived in Jerusalem. The poor lived in Bethlehem, and villages of the kind. So Bethlehem serves as a symbol both of royalty and poverty.

How else could it have been? If Jesus be Christ the King, the Chosen One of God, would not any earthly trappings of wealth or academic degrees or title look tawdry and out of place? Divine royalty entered common humanity in Bethlehem. "Though he was rich, yet for your sakes he became poor, that ye through his poverty might be rich" (II Cor. 8:9).

God's Message to You

"Fear not." Does modern man, with his massive technical achievements, need a message about fear? Or did anxiety and dread go out of date when the internal combustion engine was invented? You know well that modern man is trembling in his brightly shined boots. We in this country have often sought a material answer to man's spiritual problems. We have multiplied gadgets without end. We have achieved the highest standard of living in recorded history. And we find ourselves asking bitterly, "What shall it profit a man if he shall gain the whole world and lose his own soul?" The basic problem of our time is spiritual, and it calls for a spiritual solution. General Douglas MacArthur has well said:

> Military alliances, balances of power, leagues of nations, all in turn have failed, leaving the only path to be by way of the crucible of war. The utter destructiveness of war now blots out this alternative. We have had our last chance. If we will not devise some greater and more equitable system, Armageddon will be at our door. The problem basically is theological and involves a spiritual recrudescence and improvement of human character that will synchronize with our almost matchless advance in science, art, and literature, and all material and cultural developments of the past two thousand years. It must be of the spirit if we are to save the flesh.

"I bring you good tidings." The word "gospel" means literally "good tidings." A few centuries ago it was spelled "god-spel." Somehow the "d" dropped out, and men forget that "gospel" means stop-the-press news. Is it still news that something happened two thousand years ago? It certainly is. Christians do not rejoice over some fragments of ancient history at Christmas time. We rejoice because Christ is living and working in the world today. You have no idea how eternally new Christ is, until you have been born anew through faith in Him.

The angel brought good tidings "of great joy." There is still spiritual joy at the heart of Christmas, despite the synthetic frivolity the commercial interests have fostered. Why is Christmas a joyous season? It is a time of giving, not getting, and that is a reason for joy. It is a time when adults think about children, and actively seek their happiness. These alone would make Christmas a joyful time. But deeper far is the fact that Christmas means Christ. When you lift your thoughts to Him, fears dwindle, joys grow.

The joy stemming from our Savior's birth is promised "to all people." This follows as a matter of simple logic. Either the message of the angel is true or it is not. There is no vague point "somewhere between the extremes" about the declaration that a particular baby is to be "a Savior which is Christ the Lord." If these words are true, they are true for everybody, everywhere. If they are not true for everybody, they are true for nobody. Some will say, "Christianity is all right for us, and other people have their religion which is all right for them." Anyone who says this really means, "Christianity is wrong for us." God sent His Son to save the world.

The heart of the angel's message to you is, "Unto you is born this day in the city of David a Savior, which is Christ the Lord." In the course of the following pages we shall examine, with considerable care, the meaning of these words. The angel's message can be compressed into this one sentence. All that goes before is introduction. What follows is the only possible conclusion.

"Glory to God in the highest." When men, or even angels, sing "Glory to God," we cannot add an iota to the glory that is already His. Infinity plus one still equals infinity. But we can recognize God's glory, and express it in our hearts and lives. This is a large part of the meaning of worship. It is no favor to God when you worship Him. But He does desire your praise, as one channel through which He brings His love to bear upon your life.

"On earth peace, to men of good will." In the beloved words of the King James translation, the heavenly host sings, "good will toward men." This makes better music, but the Evangelist Luke wrote better Christianity when he said, "to men of good will." Luke wrote in Greek, where the letter "s" at the end of one word makes all that difference. Evidence points to the fact that in the days when manuscripts of the Bible had to be transcribed by hand, a careless copyist left out the letter "s." The translators in 1611 followed this copyist in preference to one who, we believe, copied accurately what the Evangelist wrote. Although we like the words the way we learned them, when we stop to think about it, Luke is right, the copyist wrong. The spiritual blessings of life are far more likely to come to the one who by God's grace is prepared to receive them. And what blessing is sought more eagerly today than peace?

During the past nineteen turbulent centuries, there has been little political peace on earth. At almost any instant you might name, somewhere man has been at war with his brother man. When there was no actual shooting, still turmoil of one kind or another existed. Tension has been the rule, not the exception. During these centuries of strife, countless men of good will have lived and worked. What does the promise of peace mean? It means, of course, that when the will of man finally is harmonized with the will of God, the only tensions of life will be those producing harmony, not discord. That time is not yet. Must we wait until then to know the peace that passes understanding?

The peace of God is a present reality in the lives of many who live today in the midst of turmoil. After his release from a Communist prison camp, a young naval aviator told a story that illustrates the actuality of Christian peace. He gave the tragic, familiar picture of starvation, torture, and brain-washing. He said there were two Christian clergymen in the camp, who seemed to form foci of resistance to the Communist appeal. So the clergymen were shot. And the young aviator, who had not been a religious man before his capture, told that every day in the camp small groups would gather, and the men would recite what verses they could recall from the Scripture. Then these men, who had every earthly reason to despair, would pray. Daily the captors would taunt, "You believe in God, why doesn't He help you?" And daily these men who had met Christ in the valley of the shadow would answer, "He is helping me."

God sent the good tidings of great joy into the world to help people to find their way through the darkness and into the light. Is He helping you? Have you received His message?

2

DO YOU NEED A SAVIOR?

> *Unto you is born this day*
> *in the city of David a SAVIOR,*
> *which is Christ the Lord.*
>
> LUKE 2:11

One day I asked a man, who is decidedly not a Christian, what he believes about Jesus Christ. He said, "I think highly of Him. He is the finest teacher the world ever saw. He gave us the Golden Rule, and if people would only follow that, the world would be heaven."

Why is this man not a Christian?

Why should he be? What is there in his idea of Christ to demand the total commitment of self that is Christianity? He sees in Jesus the world's best teacher. On that we are agreed. God sees in Him the Savior.

The Meaning of "Jesus"

The angel who brought the message to Mary said of the son whom she was to bear, "Thou . . . shalt call his name Jesus" (Luke 1:31). The name "Jesus" was often heard in our Lord's day, just as it is today. In Spanish-speaking lands many boys are named "Jesus." In English-speaking countries we spell the same name "Joshua." The name means literally "God is salvation."

23

You have a friend named Joshua. You know, in a
general sort of way, that his name means "God is salvation." When you call him on the telephone, the spiritual
meaning of Joshua's name seldom crosses your mind.
The name is the convenient label for referring to a
particular person. Just so, in Jesus' day, few of those
with whom He walked and talked realized that this
person, named "God is salvation," was God's chosen
agent to save the world.

Some ancient manuscripts of the New Testament tell
of another named Jesus. His surname was Barrabas. So
Pilate ironically offered a choice between Jesus Barrabas
and Jesus the Christ. One hoped to save the nation by
the methods of political violence. The other sacrificed
Himself to save the world.

Most names have a meaning. Seldom does a person
live to its utmost the meaning of his name, as did Jesus
the Savior.

Teacher and Savior

No Christian will argue strenuously against the idea
that Jesus is the outstanding teacher of history. But
most of us will say that teaching is not His most important work. For example, Paul and Silas were in
prison, and the warden, terrified by an earthquake,
rushed to them for help. Under similar circumstances,
what would you tell the man? You could say, truth-
fully, "Follow the Golden Rule, and you will be a
better person." But the Apostle said, "Believe on the
Lord Jesus Christ, and thou shalt be saved" (Acts
16:31). Evidently he thought the warden needed more
than ethical improvement. He needed to be lifted out of

64998

himself, up to another spiritual plane. He needed to be saved. And so does everyone else.

Teacher and Savior, what is the difference? A friend of mine is a swimming coach. He teaches the basic skills of an important art. Each summer the coach goes to a beach, where he acts as lifeguard. A coach has one set of duties, a lifeguard has a different set. My friend is able to carry out both sets of duties, but not at the same time. The lifeguard is not supposed to teach. His work is to prevent trouble, if possible. But when accidents occur, he plunges to the rescue.

Everyone agrees there should be a lifeguard at a crowded beach. The strongest swimmer agrees most enthusiastically. He says, "Of course I can take care of myself, but there are weaklings. Little children might be knocked over by a wave. Many women don't know how to swim. Some men are poor swimmers who tire easily. There must be a lifeguard, though I don't need him."

My friend the lifeguard takes an unhappy view of this attitude. He tells me that he has troubles with those who cannot swim, of course. But his most serious troubles come from those who think themselves good swimmers, and go beyond the limits of their strength. He is somewhat bitter on the subject. Last summer a close friend of his went out into the surf to rescue a "strong" swimmer, and the lifeguard lost his own life, saving one who thought he did not need to be saved.

Christianity is something like that. Jesus came into the world as our teacher. He is by long odds the finest teacher of all time, but by no means the only good one. He gave us the Golden Rule. If people would only follow it, the world would be greatly improved. How true, how obvious, and how completely stupid. The trouble is with that big "if." People do not follow the Golden Rule. Jesus was not the first to announce this great principle. Confucius said much the same thing, several centuries earlier, and people did not follow it when Confucius spoke.

Did Jesus come into the world simply to do over again what other experts had already done? If the Golden Rule did not save mankind when Confucius gave it, why should it do any better when Jesus gives it?

An important part of Jesus' total work is His teaching. But there is one part of His work that He alone could do. God has sent thousands of good teachers into the world. He has sent only one Savior. The final importance of our Savior's life is measured, not by the Sermon on the Mount, but by His sacrificial death on the cross. "God commendeth his love toward us, in that, while we were yet sinners, Christ died for us" (Rom. 5:8).

As you read through the Gospels, you find that in each of these brief biographies of Jesus something like one fourth of the entire book is given over to an account of His death. In any other biography I ever heard of, the person's death is a comparatively brief account. When most people die, their earthly life is over. When our Savior died, His earthly influence really began. He offered Himself on the cross that we might be forgiven our past sins, that we might overcome our daily temptations, that we might be changed into sons and daughters of God. He came, not to instruct us in the A B C's of morality, but to save us from our sins. So the question before us is: Do you need to be saved?

What Is Salvation?

During the last century the idea of salvation acquired a thick coating of sawdust, which pretty well obscures its importance to many intelligent people today. The most important question you ever will answer is: "Are you saved?" If, sometimes, there has been undesirable hysteria associated with the question, that does not stop it from being an important matter about which you ought to be thinking.

"Are you saved?" The question was asked of a man I know. He thought it highly amusing. He had no criminal record. His credit was good. He had never been involved in a major scandal. The whole idea of being saved struck him as being funny. "Me? Saved? I'm already here."

You cannot argue that the wretch in the gutter needs to be saved. He has sought a spiritous solution to his spiritual problems, and alcohol has become his master. As my many redeemed friends in Alcoholics Anonymous have told me, "I tried to save myself. I tried to exercise will power. But I needed a power beyond myself, to lift me out of myself." Salvation is an important issue to the down-and-outer. What of the up-and-outer? Does he need to be saved?

Here is a man, whose name is Legion. He wears good clothes. He drives a fine car. He lives in a comfortable home. He has a responsible position. He is an intelligent, attractive person. When I try to talk with him about spiritual matters, he smiles in a kind way and says, "Oh, I can be good without going to church." And that ends it, he hopes. He sees no need for the

Savior. Though he always adds, "Of course, we all make mistakes."

Mr. Legion has defined salvation as "being good." A Christian will accept that definition, if he first allows Christ to define "good." When you try to be precise about the meaning of goodness, you find yourself dealing with a slippery and elusive term. Every community has its own standards of goodness. Once I attended a trial, where a witness from one of our better penitentiaries referred to another witness as a "rat." As I understand the term, a "rat" is definitely not good. The "rat" in question was the law-abiding citizen who had given information to the police. By your standards, his action was good. By the standards of the criminal community, the same action was bad.

How good is good? If the community sets the pattern, Mr. Legion can be good, and yet harbor bitter prejudices. He can be filled with envy, hatred, jealousy, and pride, and the community will call him good — if he stays within reasonable bounds. He can snarl at his secretary and bark at his children. He can loaf on the job, or pay beggarly wages, and still someone will call him good. Jesus took considerable pains to point out the relativity of human moral standards. He showed that the publicans and harlots have their standards of good and evil. The respectable folk have their standards, which are, to be sure, a great deal higher. But the important question is, What does God call good?

It is agreed that Jesus is the supreme teacher. What does He teach about this matter of goodness?

Ye have heard that it was said by them of old time, Thou shalt not kill. . . . But I say unto you, That whosoever is angry with his brother . . . shall be in danger of the judgment. — Matthew 5:21-22

Ye have heard that it was said by them of old time, Thou shalt not commit adultery: but I say unto you, That whosoever looketh on a woman to lust after her hath committed adultery with her already in his heart. — Matthew 5:27-28

It is not enough to keep the act clean; a truly good person would keep his thoughts clean too.

Ye have heard that it hath been said, Thou shalt love thy neighbour and hate thine enemy. But I say unto you, Love your enemies, bless them that curse you, do good to them that hate you, and pray for them which despitefully use you. — Matthew 5:43-44

For us who have trouble loving our neighbors, Jesus' moral standard looks rugged and difficult. Evidently He does not think it easy to be good.

These brief quotations from Jesus' teaching are not intended as a summary. Their only purpose is to show that the Savior's standard of goodness is far higher than any of us have attained. Indeed, He summarizes His teaching on the subject by saying, "Be ye therefore perfect, even as your Father which is in heaven is perfect" (Matthew 5:48). Divine perfection is good. Less than this is not good. Thus far, I have never met anyone so completely self-satisfied as to claim that he had reached the goodness of God.

It is ridiculous to speak reverently of Jesus as the supreme teacher, if one does not pay attention to what He teaches. And the minute you examine what the teacher says, you find that you need more than instruction in righteousness; you need the Savior.

Would it be more practical to change Christ's definition of goodness, as Christians sometimes have done, or to set our standard of goodness at a height which the average person can reach by dint of much effort? Evidently Jesus did not think so. He came into the world, not to offer us more of the same thing, in a slightly improved form, but to bring something new and different. He came to introduce a new quality of life, and this is what we really mean by salvation.

Jesus said, "I am come that they might have life, and that they might have it more abundantly" (John 10:10). He was talking to people who were biologically alive, and that condition either is or is not. A person who is biologically alive simply cannot be more alive than he already is. He can be healthier, happier, stronger, or a lot of other good qualities, but he cannot be "aliver." Into the life of a person who is alive in this physical sense, our Savior introduces a new quality of life. This is spiritual life. Sometimes we call it eternal life. Perhaps the introduction of spiritual life comes with a sudden, soul-shaking religious experience. Perhaps it develops as slowly and quietly as an oak-tree. When a person has accepted the spiritual life given by Christ, then one can say that he is saved.

A person who is saved has not yet attained to Christ's standard of goodness. Indeed, he may never attain it, or even come close to it, during the earthly part of his eternal life. Biological existence comes to an end. But the new quality of life that Christ brings cannot end. It comes from God and it returns to God.

Jesus is the complete realist. Jesus is the one who is practical, not he who would make goodness easy. For Jesus looks at the whole of life, and not just the earthly part of it. He sets a standard toward which the Christian can always progress, yet He Himself is the motivating force toward reaching the standard. What is good in Christ's eyes is spiritual perfection, utter godliness in the life of a person on earth. But Christianity is not the pursuit of the impossible. Christianity is the growth of the Spirit of Christ within your life. And that is completely possible for the one who is "born of the Spirit." Christ is living and working on earth today in many hundred million lives. Few of the millions have learned to love their enemies, but some have. And all who have entrusted their hearts to Christ are growing in that direction.

Is it practical to have a goal that no one ever reaches? Near the church where I labor is a factory that produces aircraft. Many engineers and mechanics from that factory are members of the church. They tell me that their goal is absolute accuracy, but they never quite achieve it. No hole is perfectly round, no line is absolutely straight. Yet the engineers keep right on searching for perfection, and always falling short. Aircraft would be cheaper if they could just lower their standards. The whole manufacturing process would be far more relaxed and pleasant, if they could settle for errors of a few ten-thousandths, instead of reaching tolerances of a few hundred-thousandths of an inch. But if they compromise with accuracy in their work, some pilot will pay for their carelessness with his life. It is important to strive for a goal that the manufacturer never reaches. How much more is it important for the builder of a life to strive without ceasing to reach the standard of manhood as expressed in the life of Christ?

Now I am talking as if Christianity were your own achievement, a matter of pulling yourself up to heaven by your own bootstraps. Fundamentally your faith means the growth of the Spirit of Christ in your life. But if you are not striving to grow, you are not following the God-given directions for spiritual health. The Bible puts it this way, "Work out your own salvation with fear and trembling: for it is God which worketh in you" (Philippians 2:12-13). The fact that a person has accepted Christ as his Savior does not set that person free from responsibility to live a Christ-like life. Rather it is the firm ground for confidence that, in time or eternity, he will attain the goal that Christ has set.

3

A SAVIOR WHICH IS CHRIST

*Unto you is born this day
in the city of David a Savior,
which is CHRIST the Lord.*

Luke 2:11

Today the words "Jesus" and "Christ" are so closely woven together that they are interchangeable. I have talked with people who think that Christ is Jesus' last name. Even in the New Testament this fusion of terms had started to take place. So it is difficult, sometimes, for us to remember the distinction. Ideally, the name "Jesus" refers to the human life of our Lord, while the title "Christ" applies to His divine power and glory.

The Meaning of "Christ"

The burning question of Jesus' earthly ministry was, "Art thou the Christ?" (Luke 22:67). Christianity began on earth when the disciple said first, "Thou art the Christ" (Matt. 16:16). Before that time there were only followers of Jesus. After that time, there were Christians, although the word "Christian" was not coined until several years later. A follower of Jesus is one who believes that He is a capable teacher, perhaps the best teacher the world has ever seen. A Christian believes all this, and in addition he believes that Jesus is the Christ.

"Christ" is a Greek word meaning "the Anointed One." In the days of our Lord, Greek was the international language of the Mediterranean basin. Naturally the Hebrew Scripture was translated into that tongue, more than two centuries before Jesus' birth. In the Greek translation of the Bible, the word "Christ" is found many times as the equivalent of "Messiah," the Hebrew term for "the Anointed One." It was the custom, among the ancient Hebrews, to anoint a king at the time of his coronation, or a prophet at the time of his commission, or a priest when he was ordained. So "the Anointed One" means a person who has been set aside for a holy office.

Running through the Old Testament is a thread of promise that, in the fullness of time, God will send His Anointed One into the world, to be His special representative on earth. In the opening pages of the Bible we read of the conflict between good and evil, and God says to the power of darkness, "I will put enmity between thee and the woman, and between thy seed and her seed; it shall bruise thy head, and thou shalt bruise his heel" (Genesis 3:15). This cryptic sentence is God's first recorded prophecy that one day a man, born of woman, would enter into mortal conflict with evil. Though bruised in the struggle, He would stamp on the head of evil and thus destroy it. There are hundreds of similar anticipations of God's chosen representative on earth. By New Testament times it was customary to refer to these prophecies as "Messianic," that is, references to the coming Messiah, or Christ.

The Psalm of Solomon

Some fifty years before the advent of our Lord, there

appeared a remarkable poem, which today is called the seventeenth Psalm of Solomon. This is by far the most important record we have of Messianic thought in the days of Jesus. The Psalm is too long to include here in its entirety. So I have chosen some excerpts which, I hope, convey the spirit of the original.

First the poet describes the plight of the Hebrew people. Their land is invaded, morals have been corrupted:

From their ruler to the least of the people they are
    sinful;
  the king in transgression,
  the judge in disobedience,
  the people in sin.

Then the poet turns from the tragedy of the human situation to the hope that God will send the Christ:

Behold, Lord, and raise up to them their King, the
    Son of David;
  in the time which Thou, O God, knowest,
  that He may reign over Israel thy servant,
  and gird Him with strength
  that He may break in pieces them that rule
    unjustly.

He shall destroy the ungodly nations with the word
    of His mouth.
  The nations shall flee before Him at His rebuke.
  And He shall convict sinners in the thoughts of
    their hearts.

And He shall gather together a holy people,
  whom He shall lead into righteousness;
  and He shall judge the tribes of the people
  who have been sanctified by the Lord their God.

And He shall not suffer iniquity to lodge in their
    midst;
    and none that knoweth wickedness shall dwell
        with them;
    for He shall know them, that they are the sons
        of God.
And He shall purge Jerusalem and make it holy,
    even as it was in the days of old.
    And there shall be no inquity in His days in
        their midst,
    for all shall be holy, and their King is the Lord
        Christ.
He shall not put His trust in horse and rider and
    bow,
    nor shall He multiply unto Himself gold and
        silver for war,
    nor will He place His confidence in ships for the
        day of battle.
The Lord Himself is His King
    and the hope of Him that is strong in the hope
        of God.
He shall bless the people of the Lord with wisdom
    and gladness.
    He Himself is pure from sin
    so that He may rule a mighty people
    and rebuke princes and overthrow sinners
    by the strength of His word.
Who can stand against Him?
    He is mighty in words, and strong in the fear of
        God,
    tending the flock of the Lord with faith and
        righteousness

He shall suffer none among them to faint in
their pasture.

In holiness He shall lead them all.
There shall be no pride among them.
None shall be oppressed.

Blessed are they who shall be born in those days,
who shall behold the blessing of Israel
which God will bring about through the gath-
ering of the tribes.

God hasten His mercy toward Israel!
May He deliver us from the abomination to
cruel enemies!
The Lord is our King from henceforth and even
forevermore.

The Psalm tells that the Christ will be a descendant
of David, a member of Israel's royal family. He is to
rule with moral force, not military strength or political
power. He is to be free from sin. His work will be both
to sanctify His people and to destroy evil. The Psalm is
a remarkable interpretation of the Scriptural promise
about the coming Messiah. It expresses the confidence
that in God's own time He will send the Christ to earth
to save His people.

Of course there were many different understandings
of the work the Messiah would do. Some thought
He would be a military leader who would re-establish
the political independence and economic prosperity
of the Hebrews. Even after His resurrection, some of
our Lord's disciples asked Him, "Lord, wilt thou at this
time restore again the kingdom to Israel?" (Acts 1:6).
They had not yet realized what Jesus meant when He
said, "My kingdom is not of this world" (John 18:36).

Although in Jesus' day there were crude misunderstandings of the Christ's work, there were also those
who thought of the Messiah in the loftiest spiritual
terms. It was revealed to Simeon, for example, that he
would live to see the Christ; and when the infant Jesus
was brought to the temple, Simeon took Him in his
arms and said:

> Lord, now lettest thou thy servant depart in peace,
>   according to thy word:
> For mine eyes have seen thy salvation, which thou
>   hast prepared before the face of all people;
> A light to lighten the Gentiles, and the glory of
>   thy people Israel.
>
> — Luke 2:29-32

Simeon thought of the Christ as bringing light to the
people who dwell in darkness. But he warned the young
mother that her son's life would be filled with sorrow
as well as glory, and that a sword would pierce her soul.

Before Jesus was born, devout students of God's holy
Word knew that at some time God would send His
special representative to earth, that this person, the
Christ or Messiah, would be born in Bethlehem, of the
lineage of David, that His personal character would be
spotless, that He would be filled with divine wisdom
and power, that He would enter into battle with the
power of evil in the world, that after being wounded
Himself, He would emerge victorious from the battle.

Our Lord's disciples seemed to overlook the fact
that the Christ was to suffer. After the resurrection,
Jesus said to two of his friends, "Oh fools, and slow of
heart to believe all that the prophets have spoken:
Ought not Christ to have suffered these things, and to

enter into his glory? And beginning at Moses and all the prophets, he expounded unto them in all the Scriptures the things concerning himself" (Luke 24:25-27). Before Jesus' birth, the outlines of Christ's life were available to the serious student of the Bible.

It is difficult for you and me to imagine the spiritual struggle that Simon Peter went through before finally he confessed his faith that Jesus is the Christ. Before Jesus' time, and after, false "Christs" rose up and proclaimed themselves the chosen ones of God. Peter did not wish to join the ranks of the deluded people who had given their allegiance to a mock Messiah. He knew Jesus. He knew that Jesus would not deceive him. And gripped with the conviction that he could trust Jesus, he said, "Thou art the Christ." Jesus accepted the title, and said, "Flesh and blood hath not revealed it unto thee, but my Father which is in heaven" (Matt. 16:17). Today the number of those who believe that Jesus is the Christ has grown from one to several hundred million. And in each case, there has been a similar miracle of faith, as God has revealed to another of His children that Jesus is His chosen representative on earth.

Why All This Ancient History?

In New Testament times the Church rapidly overflowed the land of Palestine and expanded into the Gentile world. Gentiles had not been living in eager expectation of the coming "Christ," who would fulfill the hopes of Israel. Most of them had scarcely heard of Israel. The longings and fears of the Hebrew people were alien to their thoughts. So the sharp distinction between the terms "Jesus" and "Christ" began to be blunted. Indeed, among early Christians the title was

often misspelled as *Chrestos*. This is the happiest spelling mistake in history; for *chrestos* means "kind."
Within the next few centuries "Christ" had become a
proper name like "Jesus." Today the words are interchangeable. A person can speak of the "birth of Christ"
or about "Jesus forgiving sins." In strict accuracy,
Christ was not born, but Jesus was; and Jesus did not
forgive sins, but Christ did. Today this is a pedantic
distinction. I have not led you through this involved
discussion merely so that you will make such subtle
distinctions in the name of technical accuracy. Why
then? Does it really matter to us that Jesus is the Christ?

The Test of Truth

It matters tremendously that Jesus is the Christ, for
at least two major reasons. The first reason is the test
of truthfulness. If you make a prediction on the basis
of accepted beliefs, and the prediction comes true, you
have good reason to think that your original beliefs
were correct, and that you have followed a valid line
of inquiry. Such conclusions are not logically airtight.
There is always the possibility that you have made a
lucky guess. But the more accurate your prediction, the
smaller the chance that you have just stumbled across
the truth. This is a large part of the reason for believing
that the scientific method is one valuable means of
discovering certain kinds of truth. Scientists have made
many brilliant predictions that have been verified by
experiment. When a reputable scientist predicts something today, most of us believe that we ought to pay
strict attention.

For example, in 1846 two astronomers, Adams and
Leverrier, discovered the planet Neptune. They did

this, not by random search of the skies, but by mathematical calculation. From observed irregularities in the orbit of Uranus they concluded there must be another planet, and they calculated its orbit before it had been discovered. Telescopic observation confirmed their finding, but it did more. It demonstrated powerfully that the structure of mathematics is akin to the structure of the universe. The tools and techniques of science give reliable conclusions, when intelligently used.

So many and so wonderful have been the scientist's discoveries that some have concluded he has the only sensible approach to reality. Not many scientists have joined in this enthusiasm. They know too well that their method has limitations. Take, for example, a painting. Submit it to a scientist for examination. He can give all sorts of valuable information about the pigments and the canvas. He can tell, far better than the art critic, whether or not the painting is a forgery. He can analyze and dissect almost endlessly. But when it comes to the most important matter of all, his tools and techniques cannot help him a bit. Speaking as scientist, a person is unable to say whether a painting is a work of art or a daub. Most scientists of my acquaintance are sensitive to artistic values, but they agree that these matters are not subject to scientific tests.

We Christians believe that revelation is a valid method of knowledge, when used for its intended purpose. Through the Holy Bible, God has revealed to us what we need to know about Himself and His will. Through its pages God has answered the central question of life, "What must I do to be saved?" (Acts 16:30).

Is His answer reliable? Is revelation a trustworthy form of knowledge? Can you depend upon the spiritual guidance God gives you through His holy Word?

The Bible foretells the coming of the Christ, describes His life and work, pictures with terrifying accuracy His cross, and prophesies His resurrection from the dead. All this was written down centuries before Jesus was born. Then Jesus came into the world. Step by step, point by point, He fulfilled the prophecy. He verified the prediction. Men called Him the Christ, and He accepted the title. If all this is coincidence, it is truly a remarkable coincidence. The coming of Christ demonstrates that the biblical beliefs about God are true, that His revelation is reliable, that Christian faith is the reasonable approach to life.

The Roots of Christian Faith

The other main reason for re-examining the Old Testament meaning of Christ is as a reminder that our faith is rooted and grounded in history. Jesus took for granted the moral standards and religious teachings of the Old Testament. It is almost impossible to come to a mature understanding of the work of God in Christ, unless one has a grasp of God's work among His chosen people. Jesus was born in a context of belief and practice. Understanding His life and work demands some comprehension of the faith and life of His time, and that demands some knowledge of God's revelation that we call the Old Testament.

Sometimes Christians try to ignore the Old Testament. The attempt is not especially novel. In the second century of the Christian era there appeared a man named Marcion, who caused the church much grief.

There is no question of Marcion's sincerity. He genuinely desired to cleanse the church of all that, in his opinion, was less than Christian. There is no question of his intellectual brilliance. He was a far abler man than most of his orthodox opponents. Unhappily he neglected to notice that the major Christian virtue is love, and he chose self-denial in its stead. Not only did he abhor the theatre and the circus, but everything ornamental — even good manners. The eating of meat was forbidden. Marriage was rejected. This extreme self-denial runs counter to the Old Testament teaching that "God saw everything that he had made, and, behold, it was very good" (Gen. 1:31). Since Marcion's ideas conflicted with the Bible, he discarded all of the Old Testament and most of the New, and reinterpreted what was left. Marcion's followers were capable, sincere people. But they gradually talked their sorry scheme of things out of existence. They speculated endlessly about Christ, without recourse to the basic facts of the case as presented in the Old Testament. And finally their speculations became so vaporous that the Marcionites faded out of the picture.

Without being so honest about it, a number of Christians in the twentieth century have apparently cut themselves loose from their Old Testament moorings. Be they ever so sincere and capable, they are bound to come to wrong conclusions if they start from wrong premises. For Jesus the Christ appeared on earth within a framework of Hebrew faith and practice. To understand and apply His work, you must know something of the society in which He lived, the evils He attacked, the goods He accepted.

Jesus said of the glorious Hebrew faith, "Think not that I am come to destroy the Law, or the Prophets: I am not come to destroy but to fulfill" (Matt. 5:17). Since the Christ is the fulfillment of Old Testament faith, knowing Christ almost demands a knowledge of His background. If you understand what a person intends to accomplish, you are in a better position to find out whether or not he has accomplished it.

The faith of our fathers is sharply distinguished from the religions of the world by the picture of God that is painted in the Old Testament. In our day of juke-box religion, when the radio blares forth day and night about our big buddy up in the clouds, we need desperately the stern, majestic glory of the Holy of Hosts, as revealed in the Old Testament. It is not enough for a person to say he believes in God. What does he believe about God? The Old Testament is a centuries-long account of conflict against people who believed the wrong things about God. One of its less appetizing pages tells of a local deity named Molech, who was appeased with the slaughter of little children. Other pages tell of Ashtoreth, the goddess of fertility, who was "worshipped" by the most obscene excesses of sexual passion. The devotees of these deities believed in gods who were created by human imagination, but they did not believe in God as He reveals Himself in the Bible.

The Old Testament tells us to think of God, not as a process or influence making for good, but as a person. This is a dangerous term, easy to cheapen and abuse. But personality remains the best thought, the most god-like thought, of which the human mind is capable.

This Person is just. He makes and He enforces both the natural and the moral law. He is our Judge, but He is more than our Judge. He loves. To describe this Person, we use the pale, colorless adjective "infinite." The Old Testament says it far better:

Whither shall I go from thy Spirit?
Or whither shall I flee from thy presence?
If I ascend up into heaven, thou art there:
If I make my bed in hell, behold, thou art there.
If I take the wings of the morning,
    and dwell in the uttermost parts of the sea;
Even there shall thy hand lead me,
    and thy right hand shall hold me.
If I say, surely the darkness shall cover me;
Even the night shall be light about me.
                    — Psalm 139:7-11

Christ did not need to say this when He came to earth. It had already been said, perfectly. His work was not primarily to teach about the nature of God and of human duty. The fundamental teaching was already in the Book. He made some powerful suggestions. He cleared up some misunderstandings. He shifted several emphases. He added depth and richness and color to the biblical picture of God, but he did not change the major outlines. Christ's work was not primarily to teach. Moses and the prophets had done their part. Christ came to save.

Once you accept the fact that Jesus is the Christ, then His whole religious heritage becomes yours. Yours is the salty common sense of the Book of Proverbs. Yours is the fiery social passion of Amos. You can join in Job's cry of triumph through the tears. All these belong to him who believes that Jesus is the Christ, that the faith of the Old Testament is fulfilled in Him.

There is a large and important group of people who love the Old Testament, yet believe that the Christ has not yet come. They are the Jews. Once I asked a thoughtful Jewish friend how anyone can deny that Jesus is the long-expected Messiah. And he said, "Since you have asked me, I'll have to say that the fault is not with Jesus but with the Christians. He fills the picture well enough, but you don't. The Scripture says, 'In his days shall the righteous flourish; and abundance of peace so long as the moon endureth' (Psalm 72:7). But look at you Christians. You can't even get along with each other. What sort of peace is that? Maybe if you would start acting like Christians, I would start believing that Jesus is the Messiah. Until then, I shall continue to hope that the Messiah will come and redeem us."

Doubtless I should have had a ready retort on my lips, but I did not. I too have read a history book, about the way Christians have treated the Jews, and each other. So the conclusion of this discussion is this: it matters tremendously that the hopes and aspirations of the centuries have been fulfilled in Jesus. For you one thing matters even more — that the hopes and aspirations of the eternal Christ be fulfilled in your life.

4

THE LORD OF LIFE

> *Unto you is born this day*
> *in the city of David a Savior,*
> *which is Christ THE LORD.*
>
> LUKE 2:11

The Meaning of "Lord"

The word "Lord" means "having power or authority." It is roughly the equivalent of our word "master." In the New Testament, "Lord" is the customary term of respectful address for teachers, magistrates, doctors, and others in places of leadership. On the human level, "Lord" is a title of honor and submission. It would be strange if some had not used this title in speaking to Jesus.

Beyond the human level, the word "Lord" stands as a reverent allusion to God. The orthodox Hebrew, in Jesus' day as in our own, would not pronounce the name of God "Jehovah" or "Yaweh." Instead, when he read the sacred and incommunicable name of God, he would say "the Lord." Christians have applied the title to Christ in this latter usage. On either the human or the divine level, the title "Lord" is a mark of respect and an implied pledge of obedience.

Once Simon Peter stood before a hostile crowd and

said, "God hath made that same Jesus, whom ye have crucified, both Lord and Christ" (Acts 2:36). The Apostle was not one to use two words where one would serve. "Lord" means one thing, "Christ" means another. Briefly the distinction is this: "Christ" represents everything that God has done to redeem you. "Lord" represents what you ought to do because you have been redeemed.

Faith and Law

Christianity is a personal relationship with Christ. It is not primarily ideas about Him, nor following rules and regulations, nor belonging to an organization, nor participation in the right ceremonies. Jesus said, "This is the work of God, that ye believe on him whom he hath sent" (John 6:29). Belief "on" or "in" a person is something added to belief "about" him. For example, I believe that a certain man is a thief and a swindler. (The police share this belief with me.) I have beliefs "about" him, but I do not believe "in" him. Just so, you can hold ideas about Jesus in compartments of your mind that are hermetically sealed from the rest of your life. But this is not Christian faith. The faith that saves is personal, a relationship between persons. Any faith worth having demands some clear-cut ideas about the central person involved. Belief "on" Jesus Christ is more than these ideas. To be sure, it does mean knowing the facts and giving intellectual assent to the facts. But beyond this it means trust in the Lord, obedience to the Lord, and love for both the Lord and fellow man.

It is not enough to say the right words about Jesus. He declared with considerable candor, "Not everyone that saith unto me Lord, Lord, shall enter into the kingdom of heaven; but he that doeth the will of my Father which is in heaven" (Matthew 7:21). It is the heavenly Father's will that you believe on His Son. Belief includes more than the rational intellect. Belief includes your feelings and your decisions.

Down through the history of the Church two grievous errors have dogged our faith. One is what we call "legalism." Since a Christian must do certain things, and not do certain other things, the legalist thinks he has fulfilled his duty by observing the mere letter of the law. For example, a person gives a tenth of his income to the Lord because he believes that God demands this. This is fine and praiseworthy, as far as it goes. If he then concludes that the other nine-tenths is none of the Lord's business, he is far distant from the Spirit of Christ. Jesus speaks with scorn of those who tithe to the utmost triviality, yet neglect mercy in their daily affairs. You cannot buy the love of God by keeping a set of rules and regulations. He gave you the rules because He loves you. A Christian follows the rules because he loves God.

The opposite error is called "antinomianism." This means "disdain for the law." A person who makes this error concludes that, since God already loves him, it matters not what he does. Since salvation is a gift of God's grace and not a human purchase, some have decided that men's actions and attitudes are unimportant. No one ever found this idea in Jesus' teaching. He says, "I have given you an example, that ye should do as I have done to you" (John 13:15).

Even in New Testament times the antinomian idea had gained some ground. The Apostle Paul punctured it, presumably because it needed puncturing. "Shall we continue in sin, that grace may abound? God forbid. How shall we, that are dead to sin, live any longer therein?" (Romans 6:1,2). A Christian accepts Christ's forgiveness of sin, but he does not stop there. He accepts the Savior as Lord of his life, his Teacher, his Guide, his Example.

The legalist and the one who would discard the law are both in the wrong, because they try to separate what God has united. You can separate the sodium and the chlorine that constitute salt, but when you finish, you no longer have salt. And so, for purposes of discussion, you can talk now about a Christian's thoughts, then about his actions. But if you try to separate faith from behavior in daily life, you no longer have Christianity.

Jesus came to be our Savior. He sacrificed His life on the cross, taking unto Himself the guilt of human sin. He died that we might be forgiven. But forgiveness, though essential to salvation, is still something negative. The total program of Christianity is positive. A Christian takes Christ both as his personal Savior and his Lord. During the days of His flesh, our Lord set the example. He *told* us how a Christian ought to live, and He *showed* us how a Christian ought to live. Accepting Christ as Lord means living that way. Jesus' life was a constant fight against evil. Many of the evils He combated are still with us. I should like to examine three of the evils that Jesus attacked, and in each case raise the question: Is all this something that ended long ago, or does my Lord want me to continue the battle?

The Lord and Pain

As you read the Gospels, surely you have been impressed with the unending procession of the crippled, the blind, the diseased who hobble or are carried into Jesus' presence. Jesus did more than feel sorry for these people. He healed them. A third of the recorded miracles in the Gospels are acts of healing.

About a century ago a great divorce occurred in the western world. By silent consent it was agreed that the doctors would be concerned about the human body, and the church would care for man's soul. At its worst, scientific medicine became the human branch of veterinary science. And a good bit of what passed for Christianity was distressingly "inner." It is too soon to cheer unreservedly, but there are signs that the divorce may end in a reconciliation. Today medicine recognizes anew the importance of faith and fear, hope and hostility. Today the church is rediscovering the lost third of the Gospel. No Christian wants to go back to the pre-scientific days in the treatment of disease. That would be a strange way to thank God for men like Fleming and Osler. But we can hope and pray for the time to come on earth when all of man's wisdom will be put to work for the Lord, when faith and science will be one.

The healing of the Gadarene demoniac points a special message to us today. The healing was accompanied by destruction of a herd of swine, with great monetary loss to the owners. The record tells us that the people of Gadara came and saw the man who had been demented, sitting clothed and in his right mind; and when they understood that Jesus had cured him, they asked Jesus to go away. Instead of rejoicing in the patient's cure they rued their financial loss. Mental disease is our number one health problem today. Where proper facilities are available for treatment, there is hope for those whose minds are in the shadows. What is the story of the mental health program in your state? The typical story in this country is too many patients for the staff and equipment available. The typical explanation is, "We can't improve conditions without raising taxes, and taxes are too high already." The Lord evidently thought human sanity more important than a great deal of wealth. What are your thoughts on the matter?

It is recorded that Jesus fed those who hungered. His action is a lesson for every Christian, a lesson of care for human need. When the church goes to an area where hunger is a major problem, soon our missionaries start an agricultural school. Christians sometimes oppose such a procedure, using the argument that our mission is to preach the gospel, not crop rotation. To be sure, scientific agriculture is no substitute for the gospel. But it can be an important means of expressing our faith. To each generation of Christians falls the responsibility of using the day's wisdom to carry out the Lord's eternal purpose. And a major part of that purpose is the relief of pain.

The Lord and Prejudice

Hunger and disease have no friends on earth. Had Jesus confined His battle to these obvious evils, His life could have been tranquil. But He was not content to belabor the obvious. He went to the heart of man, and found there prejudice; and He sought to extract it.

The extraction hurts. I know. He is still removing some of my favorite prejudices.

"Prejudice" means "pre-judgment," making up your mind about a person before you have all the facts about him. We must classify people, if we are going to talk about them. Sometimes we decide that the class label tells all about the person within the class.

A Negro friend of mine tells me that he is the constant victim of a pleasant prejudice. People keep urging him to sing, on the ground that "all Negroes are musical." He would love to be musical, but he is not. Yet some of his white friends think he is hiding a light beneath a bushel. Their prejudice says that Negroes are musical, therefore this particular Negro is musical. He has experienced other, less flattering, prejudices that are equally wide of the mark.

Jesus grew up in a society that was cleft with sharp distinctions, just as is our society. Jesus aroused the fury of the prim and proper people by ignoring these man-made divisions. He often heard the sneer, "a friend of publicans and sinners." The publican of Jesus' day was a tax collector. Today the tax collector is a respected public servant. It was not so in the time of our Lord. The publican of the New Testament was a subcontractor who purchased from the primary contractor, in Rome, the right to assess and collect taxes in a particular territory. Understandably he wished to make a profit on the purchase, and the Jewish people understandably believed that the profit was exorbitant. The tax was a detested mark of subjection to an alien government. Hatred for the tax was easily transferred to the man who collected it. In other words, publicans were unpopular. In many cases, perhaps in most cases, they deserved to be. But it was prejudice pure and simple when the misdeeds of the majority were applied to every individual publican. And it was prejudice that caused the Jews to shun all tax-collectors because they thought every publican beyond the pale of redemption.

Jesus befriended the publicans. He came to earth to be the Friend of sinners, and He insisted upon loving the worst as well as the "best" sinners. Unlike some of His followers (at a distance) today, He did not descend to the level of evil people when He associated with them. Rather He raised them to His level. His friendship had a redemptive purpose. Chief among those whom He raised was the publican Matthew. Prejudice bade Jesus hate and despise Matthew. Love bade Jesus welcome him into the circle of faith. Which was the wiser policy for Him to follow? Which would be the wiser policy for you?

Far more serious, to Jesus' critics, was His love for the heretic. The Jews and the Samaritans were close together on most religious issues, sharply divided on a few. Between the two groups was a bitter hostility. The conflict began seven centuries before. There had been guilt aplenty on both sides. In the Savior's day the hatred was so intense that a Jewish traveler from Galilee to Jerusalem often would take a detour east of the Jordan, rather than travel through hostile territory. Such avoidance was not mere snobbery on the part of the Jews. There is record that sometimes Samaritans mistreated and killed Jewish travelers. Seldom in any human estrangement is all the evil on one side. And prejudice makes it almost impossible for men of good will on either side to work out a harmonious settlement.

Take the smear words of contemporary English: "hunky," "dago," "wop," "nigger," "kike," and the rest of the terms that debase the user. Roll these together, add a liberal sprinkling of contempt, and you will have a rough idea what "Samaritan" meant to most of Jesus' acquaintances. Prejudice and custom decreed that He should pass by and ignore the Samaritans. Yet the Evangelist John tells how Jesus fell into conversation with a Samaritan woman. His own disciples were startled at this shattering of prejudice. Jesus treated the woman at the well, not as a despised heretic, but as a human being. He knew that she was wrong about important religious issues. Still He took the time and trouble to listen to her beliefs. Where disagreement was necessary, He disagreed, but with charity. He did not browbeat or scold. There was no hysterical denunciation, though there had been much evil in the Samaritan woman's life. Prejudice bade Jesus to ignore the woman at the well. The heavenly Father bade Him to show her the Way and the Truth and the Life.

Surely it means something to you and me that Jesus defied prejudice in the days of His flesh. There is no special merit in our beaming approval upon His actions two thousand years ago. His action should serve as an example for us to follow today.

The Lord and Pride

Had Jesus been content to help the suffering and to break down prejudice, still He might have escaped the cross. For everyone who has read the Old Testament ought to know that prejudice is wrong. God loves the

people of the world, not just the members of this or
that charmed circle. But Jesus smashed through the
outer defenses of the soul, and at the heart of religious
man He found pride. Exposing this pride cost Him
His life.

It was the conflict with the scribes and the Pharisees
that brought Jesus to His death. And this conflict is
easily misunderstood today. The scribes were the pro-
fessional copiers of the Hebrew Scripture. The Pharisees were the outstanding interpreters of the faith.
When we hear the word "Pharisee" we automatically
think "hypocrite." So thinking, we miss the whole point
of what Jesus is saying. Through the scribes and Pharisees, Jesus tells us that religious people in every generation are in danger of being destroyed by their own
self-satisfaction. Religious people, today as two thousand
years ago, have a truly remarkable capacity to be pleased
with themselves.

From the human viewpoint the scribes and Pharisees
were the best people in Jerusalem. By the standards of
Jerusalem, or of your home town, they were good, law-
abiding, moral pillars of the community. I have seen
Christians grow red in the face, denouncing the ancient
Pharisees who are no longer here to protect themselves.
But the sins that are so visible in the Pharisee are still
in the world. If they were evil yesterday, doubtless they
are evil today.

Jesus points out many sins of the scribes and Pharisees that have a contemporary sound. There is the
matter of substituting ceremony for charity. He does
not admire the pious show, to impress the neighbors.
He is distressed when men are so busy arguing their

faith that they forget to live it. He is appalled at religious man's capacity to swallow camels while gagging at gnats. His heart breaks when he sees religious people "devour widows' houses and for a pretense make long prayers" (Mark 12:40). The observances and ceremonies of faith are helps toward godly living. When used as a screen for godless actions, these practices become dangerous.

The Pharisee stood and prayed thus with himself, God, I thank thee, that I am not as other men are, extortioners, unjust, adulterers, or even as this publican. I fast twice in the week, I give tithes of all that I possess.

— Luke 18:11,12

On the surface this catalogue of virtue is true. The Pharisee was not like other men. He faithfully observed the rules and regulations of spiritual life. He was generous with his wealth. And he was deeply gratified with himself. If we would profit from Jesus' comments about this Pharisee, we need to look in the mirror and ask, "Lord, is it I?" Asking this question is painful, especially when the Lord answers, "Yes, it is you."

Jesus knew the Pharisees with all their faults even better than we do, but He did not shun them. On doctrinal matters He agreed with them more often than not. He was a welcome guest in the homes of some Pharisees. Many of the sect were sincere in their questioning Him. In the life of every man is the seed of pride. In the lives of some Pharisees this seed had grown into a luxuriant parasitical destroyer. The Lord pointed out the error of the Pharisees so that they might forsake it, and you and I might avoid it.

"Except your righteousness shall exceed the righteousness of the scribes and Pharisees, ye shall in no case
enter into the kingdom of heaven" (Matthew 5:20).
It is not difficult to be a better person than we usually
imagine the Pharisee to have been. As far as you and I
are concerned, we had better forget to think "hypocrite" every time we hear the word "Pharisee." There
is no use throwing stones at dead people. The Bible is
God's word to us, not a book of ancient history. Jesus,
in His searing indictments against the scribes and
Pharisees, is addressing you and me, saying, "Unless
you are better than the best, unless God is working in
you to guide and control your striving, you cannot
reach the goal." You need more than your own striving. You must be saved. Yet being saved must include
endless striving to become a person like your Savior.

It is always easier to talk than to act. Jesus tells us,
through the Pharisees, to beware of the temptation to
be proud. But our Lord is not content just to show
where the wrong lies. He leads in the paths of righteousness. At the Last Supper the Savior rose from the table
and girded a towel about Himself. He poured water
into a basin, and washed the feet of His disciples. In
the hot, dusty land where He lived, a wealthy person
would provide a servant to wash the feet of his guests.
This was considered a warm expression of hospitality.
It was always deeply appreciated by the guest. What
the servant thought of the custom is not recorded.
Jesus Christ, King of Kings and Lord of Lords, knelt
at the feet of unworthy men and rendered humble
service to them.

A Christian must take to heart the Savior's words,

"I have given you an example, that ye should do as I have done to you." Jesus has set the example, in terms of compassion for human need, in acts of love for sinful men, in shattering the tabus that divide man from man, in tearing down pride and practicing humility. When you call Him "Lord" you pledge that, by His grace, you will follow the example He has set.

5

WHAT THE ANGEL DID NOT SAY

And Thomas . . . said unto him,
My Lord and my God.

JOHN 20:28

When the shepherds had heard the chorus of angels, they wisely decided to go to Bethlehem and see for themselves. All they saw was a baby. But the child grew, in wisdom and in stature and in favor with God and man. From infancy, men called Him "Jesus." In His early maturity, many hailed Him as "Lord." One by one, His followers came to acknowledge Him as the "Christ." Is there anything left to say?

After Jesus' resurrection, His followers began to discover that their eyes had been closed to the full glory of their Lord. They knew they had walked and talked with God's promised Messiah. Gradually the conviction filled the church at large that men had walked and talked with God.

We use the Latin word "Incarnation" to express the mystery of God-with-us. This is a compound word. The preposition "in" has the same meaning in Latin as in English. The noun *carnis* means "flesh." So the word "incarnation" means the appearance of someone "in the flesh." Christians spell the word with a capital "I," to refer to the embodiment of God in Christ.

61

The Mystery of the Incarnation

The Incarnation is a mystery. To mention only the more obvious difficulties about this belief, God is everywhere, and Jesus had to be in only one place at a time. God is all-wise, and Jesus "grew in wisdom." God is unchangeable, and Jesus changed, from a little baby into a man, from a healthy man into a bloodless corpse, from a dead body into the vibrant, radiant Victor over sin and death. There are so many difficulties about belief in the Incarnation that in almost every age of Christian history some have denied that God was in Christ. In the early days it was the Arians. At the time of the Reformation it was Servetus. Today it is the Unitarians. And along with those who openly and honestly deny the Incarnation, there are some who have refused to make up their minds about the matter.

Why does anyone hold to a belief that simply bristles with intellectual difficulties? Why have the overwhelming majority of Christians, down through the ages, held that Christ is God? Why have we not been able to accept the obvious truth, that Jesus was a very, very, very good man, and then get on with the business of living out his teaching?

The majority of those who have tried the experiment of Christian living have joined with the Apostle Thomas. Men call him "Doubting Thomas." He had grave intellectual difficulties with the Christian faith. But he had also a deep personal loyalty to his Lord, and he followed Jesus when others wanted to run away. He knew that our Lord was crucified, and he knew that death is a one-way street. So when his friends told him that Jesus was risen from the dead, Thomas came to the sensible conclusion that they were suffering from an hallucination. Even so, he continued to be part of the society that was united in love for Christ; and when the risen Lord appeared again to that society, it was Thomas the "skeptic" who said, "My Lord and my God."

Belief in the Incarnation came to Thomas as a matter of Christian experience. Thomas was so overwhelmed by the impact of his Lord's personality that he concluded, "I have walked and talked with God." This was long before the Incarnation was a doctrine of the Church; even before there was any written New Testament to teach such a belief, or to cast light on the Old Testament prophecy of this miracle. And ever since that time, the facts of Christian experience have led men to accept the revelation through Scripture that "God was in Christ reconciling the world unto Himself."

Belief in Jesus, the ethical teacher, has proved to be a point of departure rather than a point of arrival in the spiritual pilgrimage of mankind. A person who tries to stop there usually finds himself moving on. Sometimes he wanders farther and farther from Jesus, the teacher of ethics, until he has nothing left but a vapid humanism. But during the past quarter century, we have seen some of the most searching, critical minds of the church taking the other way. Starting with Jesus the man, they have been drawn deeper and deeper into the mystery of His being, until they have united with Thomas in the cry of faith, "My Lord and my God."

It is difficult to believe in the Incarnation, but one thing is even more difficult, and that is to deny the Incarnation, while still taking Jesus seriously.

During the past century every major belief of the
Christian church has been subject to savage, destructive
criticism. Sometimes Christians have trembled, thinking their faith in danger. If you believe that Jesus
Christ triumphed over the cross, you need not fear His
ability to survive critical examination today. Once it
was fashionable to believe there never was such a person as the Jesus of history, that He was a myth, like
Santa Claus, begotten of a pathetic desire that such a
man might be. This idea collapsed under its own
weight after a while. Scholars continued and intensi-
fied their search for the rounded historical outlines of
the Savior's earthly life. Thanks to their studies, every
Christian today can see Jesus, the Man of Galilee, more
clearly than could our fathers. But the outstanding
discovery of a century's ruthless examination of Christian faith is: The more intensively you search for the
full truth about Jesus, the more clearly does it appear
that you must accept the mystery of His divine personality.

Many who are not Christians tell us they can accept
the divinity of Christ. A Hindu friend of mine is glad
to say that our Lord is divine, then he explains, "All
men are divine, and in Jesus the divinity was less
shrouded than in most of us." Some who call themselves Christians will say that the divine spark dwells
in every man, and in Jesus this spark was fanned to a
flame. Orthodox Christianity rejects these facile explanations and says: Before all worlds began, God was,
and when all worlds have ended, God will be eternally
the same, Father, Son, and Holy Spirit. God the Son,
God of God, Light of Light, very God of very God,

begotten, not made, entered into the whirlpool of human existence. The Eternal was compressed into time. The Infinite humbled Himself to accept finitude. God became man and dwelt among us, and we crucified Him.

No Christian wishes to be gullible. Nobody wishes to believe something just because it has been believed for a long time. Men believed for centuries that the earth was flat, and they called on the Bible to "prove" their contention. We have discarded such reasoning upon the basis of further study. The belief did not square with the facts. At the same time, the facts of the case have compelled more and more Christians to believe, with Thomas, that Christ is God. Jesus said, "Blessed are they that have not seen, and yet have believed" (John 20:29). In every nation on earth today are some who share this blessing. Still, remembering the difficulties of Thomas, those of us who in faith have accepted the mystery of the Incarnation should be slow to condemn those who have not yet reached such a belief. Perhaps our most valuable contribution would be living such lives that those about us would be forced to conclude that God Himself has transformed and redeemed us. A Christian life is the unanswerable argument for Christian faith.

The Bearing of the Incarnation

Once I was speaking about the mystery of the Incarnation, and in the discussion that followed, a man rose and asked, "If, as you say, Christ was God, what difference does it make?" This man had accepted Jesus as the teacher of morals. He was sincerely trying to follow Jesus, but he honestly thought that theology has woven a web of dogma about Jesus, so dense and so obscure that men cannot see the religion of Jesus because of the religion about Jesus. He thought the doctrine of the Incarnation a hindrance, not a help, to essential Christian faith.

It is a fair question, "What difference does it make?" Christians ought to ask themselves that question about every doctrine of the faith. Assuredly God embodied Himself in the person of Jesus to make a difference in your life. What difference?

Religious history is filled with fables about some god coming to earth in mortal form. And what happened when he got here? Zeus, for instance, used to make a fairly regular practice of that sort of thing, and he usually ended by falling in love with some mortal woman and committing adultery with her. Sincere, devout people of ancient Greece tried to make allegorical explanations of such fables until they gave it up as a bad job, and accepted the mystery of God's Incarnation in Christ. They reasoned that God could not possibly be as bad as fabled Zeus. Then they feared that God could not possibly be as good as Jesus. Yet they rejected one incarnation as myth, and accepted the Incarnation of Christ as history. What difference does it make? In Christ one can see the moral purity of God acted out in human life.

Religious thought has always been plagued with a major dilemma. Any terms we may use to describe God are inadequate. Our language originates in the world of space and time. God is beyond space and time. So, in speaking about God, we must use a language that cannot express exactly what we mean. The Psalmist says, "Bow down thine ear, O Lord, hear me"

(Ps. 86:1). He knows that God does not have "ears," and does not "hear" as you and I do. But how better could you express what the psalmist wishes to say?

God can most accurately be described in negatives: "immortal," "invisible," "incorruptible." But after one has negated long enough, he is left with what philosophers call the undifferentiated Absolute. And it is rather difficult for most of us to respond to an infine Zero in the heavens. The story is told of a monk with the Zen Buddhists, who asked his superior to tell him about God. The superior answered by kicking the young man. This was an effective, though not completely charitable, way of saying that God is beyond description, that man cannot talk sensibly about God, and therefore ought to keep silent.

You can talk about Jesus. You can talk about His kindness, His friendliness to little children, His compassion for the sick, the helpless, the hungry. You can talk about Jesus' concern for those on the other side of the fence, the heretic and the outcast. You can talk about Jesus' hatred of sham and mock piety. You can talk about Jesus' love for the sinner, of the way He sacrificed Himself to save the sinner. You can adjust your life to the life and teachings of Jesus, and this is a considerable difference. With the life of Jesus before him, the Christian can know a great deal about the nature and the will of God.

Does it matter that God in Christ entered the vortex of human experience, that God knows what it means to be sucked under and destroyed? It makes all the difference in the world. My work as pastor brings me into daily touch with those who suffer. Recently I talked with a man who was stricken with an incurable ailment at the peak of his usefulness in the world. We would say that the world needs his kindness, his patience, and his technical skill. Today he has reached a place where sedatives no longer ease his pain, and he asked me, "Why do things like this happen when God is love?" The question is nothing new, God knows. Job asked it, and his friends failed to provide him a tenable answer. Some have decided that, since there is much pain in the world, there is no over-all purpose, no pattern, no plan, no God. But some of us have found Christ dying on a cross. We who believe in the Incarnation know that God has entered completely into man's lot. God Himself has explored human misery.

Does it make any difference that Christ has suffered and known the pangs of death? It means that there is no pain on earth that God does not share. It means that God is no mere spectator of the human tragedy. He has chosen to be the central participant in the vast drama. Each human life comes to an end, usually in pain. Finally all human life will end. But Christians know that beyond the cross is the Resurrection.

Still I have not answered my friend's question, "Why do things like this happen?" I do not know the answer. But I do know that my friend is finding strength to endure his pain through the knowledge that God understands and cares when men suffer. Our Savior's suffering was no accident in history. God took the cross and transmuted man's failure into victory. But He did not direct this spiritual alchemy from outside. Christ Himself is both Victim and the Victor, and He offers the final victory of life to each who suffers today.

God and the Cross

Christians have always believed that the chief importance of the Incarnation lies in the forgiveness of sins. The fact of sin is central to human tragedy. Man is caught in a snare of his own creation, and his efforts to release himself only bind him closer. Every serious religion in the world deals with the basic fact of man's alienation from God. Man as he is and man as he ought to be are far apart. We Christians see that guilt is what separates man from God. And what can man do to atone for his guilt?

The usual answer to the problem of guilt is "good works." Say so many prayers, give so many alms, make a pilgrimage to a holy place — this sort of thing is supposed, somehow, to erase a sinner's guilt. The answer is not good enough. Take for example a clear-cut instance of moral evil. A person intentionally drives his car through a traffic signal. What can he do to atone for the wrong he has done? If he places his reliance on good works, he will diligently observe all traffic signals for the rest of the day. As any policeman will assure you, this is not enough. A person ought to obey traffic signals. By doing his duty, he cannot escape responsibility for a past failure to do his duty. Jesus set the standard of human duty, "Be ye therefore perfect, even as your Father which is in heaven is perfect" (Matthew 5:48). One who has fallen short of this standard on Monday can scarcely change the fact by stretching toward it on Tuesday.

A person cannot erase his own guilt. Can another person erase it for him? Centuries before the time of Christ, Moses tried and he failed. Moses was leading

his unruly people through the desert. He went up into
the mountain to commune with God. They stayed be-
low in the desert and communed with the devil. When
Moses came back to camp, his hopes and ideals were
shattered. The people had sinned. His first reaction
was anger. Then his love for the people began to
overcome his anger, and he said:

> Ye have sinned a great sin: and now I will go up
> unto the Lord; peradventure I shall make an
> atonement for your sin. And Moses returned unto
> the Lord, and said, Oh, this people have sinned a
> great sin, and have made them gods of gold. Yet
> now, if thou wilt forgive their sin —; and if not,
> blot me, I pray thee, out of thy book which thou
> hast written. And the Lord said unto Moses, Who-
> soever hath sinned against me, him will I blot out
> of my book.   — Exodus 32:30-33

Moses, one of the strongest men God ever created,
offered himself as a substitute for his people. He
offered his immortal soul in exchange for the souls of
those under his leadership. He offered to bear the
burden of their guilt. Greater love hath no man than
this. Yet God turned down the offer. Among the spiritual and intellectual giants of all time, Moses looms
gigantic. Yet God knew that Moses was not good
enough, not strong enough to atone for the sins of other
people. If Moses could not bear such a burden, who can?

God can lift a load that is too heavy for any man,
and so God Himself came into history, and lived a fully
human life, in order that a man might bear the load
that is too heavy for men. The divine Savior did not
find the burden of human guilt easy to bear. It crushed

Him and stifled Him. It drove a wedge between Him and His Father; so that the divine Son of God cried out, "My God, my God, why hast thou forsaken me?" (Matthew 27:46). Only when Christ dwelt among men there was one on earth strong enough, wise enough, good enough to carry the burden of human guilt, to take it from the heart of the sinner and into His own heart.

Does it make any difference that God came down? In a world that is arming to destroy itself, does it matter that Christ has shown God's love to be indestructible? Does it matter that Jesus has shown that human pain has meaning and purpose? Does it matter that God has acted in history to bring forgiveness for your sins?

It matters. It makes a difference that God was in Christ. To you who dwell in the valley of the shadow, there is one Light that man cannot extinguish. To you who are tortured by guilt comes the offer of divine forgiveness and peace. Before you who flounder in search of moral direction lies the Way and the Truth and the Life. You who weep at the loss of one beloved can rejoice that Christ has won the final victory over death. You who feel lost and alone can receive the strengthening assurance, "Lo, I am with you alway, even unto the end of the world." Your life has meaning and purpose. Your life is so important that "the Savior which is Christ the Lord" went to a cross to redeem you. And who is this Savior? Though He is man, He is more than the best of men. Though He is teacher, guide, and example, He is more. When all else is shaken, this fact can never be changed, that God came down to draw you up to Himself.